Second Sight

poems by

Daryl Hafter

Finishing Line Press
Georgetown, Kentucky

Second Sight

Copyright © 2025 by **Daryl Hafter**
ISBN 979-8-88838-906-5 First Edition
All rights reserved under International and Pan-American Copyright Conventions. No part of this book may be reproduced in any manner whatsoever without written permission from the publisher, except in the case of brief quotations embodied in critical articles and reviews.

ACKNOWLEDGMENTS

Special thanks are due to Eric Wayman for help and encouragement and to Micah Warschausky for technal support, to Rose-Anne Donner Colt for close and sensitivel reading and to Beth Israel Congregation, Ann Arbor, MI, for giving these poems a home.

Publisher: Leah Huete de Maines
Editor: Christen Kincaid
Cover Art: Naomi Hafter
Interior Artwork: Daryl Hafter
Interior Photos: Naomi Hafter
Author Photo: Amy Barnett
Cover Design: Elizabeth Maines McCleavy

Order online: www.finishinglinepress.com
also available on amazon.com

Author inquiries and mail orders:
Finishing Line Press
PO Box 1626
Georgetown, Kentucky 40324
USA

Table of Contents

Reading Scripture 1
    Learning the Haftarah 3
    Hanukkah Candles.. 4
    Genesis.. 6
    The Divine Gamble: A Theological Debate................. 7
    A New Year Song 9
    The Happy Newborn Year 10
    An Old Woman in the Exodus from Egypt 11
    Omer Rhymed 12
    Counting the Omer.. 13
    Is It All Right to Read the Torah If You're Not So
        Sure About God? 14
    The Best Possible World 16

Walking the Neighborhood 17
    Neighborhoods 19
    Still Sunday... 20
    A Covid Walk... 22
    Covid Spring 24
    Death of a Friend... 26
    My Garden of Eden 27

Awakening 29
    Green 31
    Ballad of an Autumn Tree 33
    In the Thinking of My Heart...................................... 35
    The Search 36
    The History of London 37
    The Old Ones 38
    Sadness... 40
    Gathering 40
    The Funeral 40
    Shiva 40
    Alisa 41
    Consolation 46

Reading Scripture

Learning the Haftarah

In tenth century Yemen
    a boy was reading
Right to left
And singing as he read.
He grew up hearing song
    with script.
His elders chanted prayer,
      from ancient time.
On the page, the melodies were spelled as one,
vowels next to trills.
No possible confusion,
    That's how it was.

I, coming late to learn,
      had always followed
        Left to right.
Songs were separate, bundled with a choir.
Reading, in a chair,
    alone.
How could there be a tie
    To one, twelve centuries ago?
It's like prehistory to me!

But listening to the chant,
the words would be bereft without the song.
I grab the melody.
I am that boy in Yemen!
    Right to left.

Hanukkah Candles

Winter planting
 fills bronze cups
with colored stalks.

On our mantel's window box
we force eight marigolds
into brief bloom,
and catch the buttercup glow
of matchlight
on our cheeks.

Praise for the miracle
of light.
Praise Spring in Wintertime,
the gift of petals on the snow
and oil from an empty urn.

Genesis

Genesis
could have been
a fireworks show,
sparks flaring
through an inky sky
to die in blackness
till the Lord
revived the spectacle.

Instead
creation held
the master plan.

Pebbles know
how to grow into trees.
Grains of sand
are seeds for flowers,
and earth produces
human folk.

Matter,
sacred as spirit,
lives God's dream:
I am that I am.

The Divine Gamble: A Theological Debate

Once upon a time
before there was time
A Great Awakening rumbled the heavens.
God said, "I want my people!"
       I want to show my power,
 to have the people
celebrate my might
and know I can't be touched or seen.
I want their good behavior and their praise."

                                               "Oh," said a voice,
                                                  "You want to stay invisible,
                                                       unformed,
                                                         untouchable,
                                                      but they should be material?
                                           Who's idolizing who?"

"Don't be impertinent," said God.
"They'll learn the rules of charity
and with belief
they'll come to praise me as their own."

                                        "Ah," said the voice in quizzical rebuke,
                                             "The praise of angels, not enough?"

"You're still impertinent," said God.
"And when they go astray?"
"I will be there to talk."
                                      "But will they listen?"

 "There'll be a guidebook, with examples from their history."

                                      "They'll disappoint, they'll disobey"

"They will invent. They will delight"
                                      "That's not enough. It's a mistake!"

"No! Never a mistake. It is a wager!"

A New Year Song

Who would have thought
to find
beginning in an end?
A new year when the crops have come,
the flowers turned to seed,
the welcome green now shed
upon the ground
in gold and red.

Why not a new year
in the Spring,
whose yearning promise
leads us on without a care,
the very kernel
yet to burst into maturity?

Why not a song of mourning
when we mourn?
It is another ending
is it not?
When fullness withers down
From cheer and robust life,
Like spent apples in a sack.

It is our task to gather up the seed,
to hold our faith
beyond the barren soil,
to celebrate, to plant,
to find beginning in an end.

The Happy Newborn Year

The Lord sat down in a regal chair
Whose shape we cannot know
Behind a curtain of Holiness
Where mortals may not go.

Looked at the creatures and the fields
He'd labored to create
And gave them each a distinctive rite
To help them celebrate.

    And the hills skipped
Like rams,
    And the little brooks
Like lambs.
    And the poplar forest
Shimmered in the breeze
    As a wave of glitter
Rustled through the trees.

And the leaves collected dew,
A second miracle come true,
Sprayed that moisture in the air
Till it coated every hair
Of the beings gathered there.

Even the caterpillar hanging free
Wove his own lace around a tree.
As the maples swayed ahead
And flashed from green to red,
While the oak trees turned around
Forgot their roots were in the ground.

Hailing Creation as the Word,
Praising and honoring the Only Lord,
When Deed and Name were one,
And the universe was begun.

An Old Woman in the Exodus from Egypt

Fearful
I am fearful
   Of this plan
      To forge the desert
Rushing out
     Into the unknown
        Where wild beasts and famine may lie in wait.
Oh, the young
   Are all for it.
Well, it's they who catch the overseers' lash.
They seek a future of their own.
   They do not see the troubles on the way.
  Do they think Egyptians
    Will not wake from their oblivion,
   And send an army after us?
       A horde that claims back the gold they gave.
      A Pharoah, whose mind is ever changeable.
     A people, whose memory of plagues recedes,
       and with resentment turns to cruelty
         and torments the fallen stragglers.

What shall I do? Go out and face the unknown,
   Or stay and bear a country's retribution?
Shall I go along and be the unheroic one.
   Not to complain,
Only to lay my bones and be forgotten on the way.

May this rag-tag band find the path
   To following a world of laws,
    To praise the God we cannot see.

Omer Rhymed

I should call a man in California
But I think I'll write a poem instead.

I should go outside and weed the garden
But I think I'll write a poem instead.

I should start to read my French homework
But I'd rather write a poem instead.

I should put away the dishes on the shelf
But I need to write a poem instead.

I forgot to sweep the kitchen floor
I was writing a poem instead.

The soup boiled over in the pot
My words got tangled in a knot.

The sheets were rumpled on the bed,
I was rhyming out the Omer in my head.

Counting the Omer

How do we use our days?
This Time which seems to shrink
   as we use up more of it?
We let our daily chores
  fill up the hours
    like sand flowing through our hands.
But sand moves through a measuring glass
   as well.
And time that cradles us
   will not be caught to stay.

How can we manage?
   Balancing between the great galactic sweep
and our minute share of it?

The Omer's reeds will help,
   Reminding us that as each day appears,
thin as wheat stalks, destined to decay,
but ours, countable, and to be filled with praise.
Within the inexorable rushing flow
   We'll catch the time to plant.

Is It All Right to Read the Torah If You're Not So Sure About God?

Aren't you curious
   About the history of a people,
     Said to be the first to have
A god you cannot see?

It's not a glamourous tale, you know.
Free will isn't always charged with piety.
Deceit and trickery
             Self-serving acts and treachery
Are in the mix.
And on this group, strict rules are laid.

As they evolve from fearful herders
   To sophisticated actors
      Among the nations,
Still carrying their human disabilities.

Aren't you curious
  To take the story
     As far as it will go?

The Best Possible World

Rabbi Eliezer said, "If God had wanted a sinless world, it could not be a world."

No sins,
No Torah.

No Torah,
No Story.

No Story,
No lessons.

No lessons,
No rules.

No rules,
No order.

No order,
No creation.

I asked, "Wouldn't it be better if men and women were more like each other?"

My friend answered, "No, it's more interesting this way."

And maybe God felt the same.

Walking the Neighborhood

Neighborhoods

"We really only build for ourselves,"
    the architect reported.

Trail the winding stairway
        up the outside wall.
Plant a darling tower on the roof.
          Adorn the house with peaks
          and little balconies
because we love the scene with
        Romeo and Juliet.

And then we leave.

That fanciful cupola now hides
    behind pine trees.
A jumbled roof no longer beautiful,
      balconies weighed down
          with dirt and vines.

I walk by, wishing I could see
        a sweeping roof, a window
          fronting on the view.
I wonder what they had in mind,
    those owners,
when wooden planks that had been
    elegant in a tree
waited, hoping that their next employ
      might please as well.

Still Sunday

Is there room for a quiet poem
        Without the monsters and the smell of death?
        All disjointed,
              shocks uncovering the cruel and dangerous at the end.

Is there time for a quiet Sunday?
        As little legs pump down the street
        And grownups find ridiculous modes of transport—
            Peddling prone or sitting in a box with wheels,
            Motored scooters and bikes with ankles flapping.

Autumn trees float yellow flakes, confetti in my hair
to celebrate the day
    And still air pauses
           with a hint of storm.

We say to one another,
        It won't last.

Notice how this cracked egg shimmers,
beautiful alone.

A Covid Walk

Today there's sun
to brighten up
the trees that last month were feathered out with leaves.
Now gaunt, dark
sentinels,
                                  unwelcoming.
They throw their shadows down
and keep the snow beneath that shaft
 alive and cold.

I must watch the sidewalks
carefully.
And with surprise, I find a roster of the neighborhood—
        embossed in concrete, the history of the town.
 The concrete makers have put their names and dates into the walk.
      I can judge the quality of their work:
A.O. Thompson 1923, still sturdy
                      WPA, 1940, smooth and bold
                      Anderson & E. Blitz, 1973, rough with gravel
                      WAT, 1985, already crumbling
A path with skill and faults built in.

But stop!
Ice there.
       How to safely walk?
Just then a truck pulls up.
       The driver stops.
"Can I help you?"
          With his brown hand, I get across the ice.

I cry all the way home.

Covid Spring

We worried Spring
   would forget us this year.
Those stick trees,
   dark and tight,
listening to the soil
and not to us.

Like ancient Romans
we thought to light some candles
   to remind the sun to stay.

Now bursting out,
this green
   that fills the sky,
pays no attention to our woes.
Doesn't Nature know
what we've been through
and still endure
   as air brings plague and grief?

We're tossed inside
   a great bowl.
Catch a cloud,
plant a seed,
pluck a flower.

Death of a Friend

They said the trunk was hollow
        Inside
And it had to come down.
An old friend
   Now become an enemy,
Poisoned inside by old age,
   I guess.

But not without a fight!

It takes three trucks
   Jamming up the road.
Five men,
      Wary, stand aside
      and run away from falling branches,
culled by the tall steel robot and the man safe inside his cabin.
He's not daring to approach without a shield!

The sawing man
      cuts chunks of the fat trunk.
        It cries, "Ohh, Ohh, as the steel cuts in.
I'll not give up without a fight.
Watch out for my huge body floating down."

They brought their biggest jaws
to cart away the last round parts.
And now, just the trunk is anchored to the ground.
It lifts a lewd finger up
      to make a final show.

"Grind the rest of me to make compost,
      but here I stand,
       older than you mortals
       ever will."

My Garden of Eden

Meg asks me what I wish for,
   what I couldn't live without,
      my Paradise, my Garden of Eden.

I answer: It's the gift of speculation,
     of learning how things go together.

I hold my breath,
Beside that door to happiness.
You know what became of Eve
   who wanted knowledge of the universe?

Open, it might unleash
those slippery evil crawling things,
      that stain perfection.

I don't care!
I want a finer net
    to troll the depths of oceans
and bring up things unknown.
My Garden of Eden is a pool of wonderment.

Awakening

Green

Green,
  I love you green
      When springtime fringe comes tinted,
          light with yellow.

And when the rush of leaves
    bursts forth,
        Overnight the trees are canopied.

Sheltering the summer flowers
          and grass,
  Green wraps a verdant world.

Come Autumn, leaves blaze
    Before deserting black arms and trunks.

We seek out pines,
    Our promise of another year.

Ballad of an Autumn Tree

My Love, the wind,
  comes when it will
      to fill my many arms.
                I'm like an octopus;
                      the wind like water,
                      can't be caught.
      And when it flows
                  we bounce and bend together.
Perhaps we do create, like parents joining.

Or is it just a dance?
Orange so vibrant it's almost pink.
Red with purple underneath.
And yellow leaves,
    A momentary sun.

The untamed wind finds guidance in prickly red hawthorn leaves
to twist and shake
                frivolous
                      against
                              a straight-laced poplar.
But oh, the generous maple. Still standing green!
    Outdoes us with chiffon that turns and waves.

It is a symphony,
      A waltz that sweeps across the sky,
in full embrace.

In the Thinking of My Heart

In the thinking of my heart
I reach
a place that's deep in space,
without a fence, nothing, nothing there
or something earlier than air.

In the thinking of my heart,
 that's close inside
to breathe alongside you,
 to stretch in your hard reach,
To know how you measured
and why.

In the thinking of my heart,
 there is no gulf
between a thought and joy.
The thought is joy,
the deep is near,
the wonder is made real
as it opens,
 opens
 to me.

The Search

Child, are you playing
hide and seek with me?
   Come out, come out wherever you are.
Don't you remember any childish games?

I look for you in corridors of marble.
        Cool, rational places
            That were never meant to be playhouses.
Or in gardens at the hallway's end
faded roses and ivy cascading Italian statues.
Are you there, hiding behind a satyr's frozen leer?

The heavy air
presses me out of the stone patio
and through the iron gate.
Too still for anyone to live in that enclosure.
It would embalm
a figure seated for a moment
and leave her posed
forever
on a garden bench.

Come out, come out.
    Squeeze through the iron railings of the fence
and leave that silent game
        where you sit, like Lot's wife but turned to stone,
marble hand caressing a Pompeian form
whose flesh has sifted into air,
waiting for a friend who will not breathe again.

The History of London

Only the names of streets
remain
and some low spires informing us
that what was once considered great
is now made quaint
by glass and steel.
The rest is written down,
if kept at all
  on nothing more concrete than sheets
and sheets of paper.
The arrogant imperialists,
        prudent shopkeeper,
and rogue
alike enrolled and tabulated.

Their lives,
once ragged with desire and toil,
are now compressed into abstract significance for us,
labeled, classified, and made solemn.

We think we do them proud.
        But I hear a babel of complaint
from crushed and splintered skulls
beneath the road,
strange accents, uneasily confined to our flat prose.

They wish to speak again!

The Old Ones

The old ones
live scattered through towns
buying bread and morning papers from the neighborhood grocers
 and pacing out the small advantages that come to hand.

What have they to do with graves
 placed close as bricks upon a wall
and tenements of gravestones bounded by an iron fence
that separates uncaring factories
from an oasis of the past?

The weighmaster calls:
    Who has eighty? Who has ninety?
And the old ones flinch,
pretend they did not hear.
But he sees the telltale owning of that burden.
He calls them
and they find their path.
Frowning and resentful, they go where beds are laid,
each drawn to a narrow couch,
and on the mound sink down,
still muttering through sunken cheeks, their white hair wild with anger.

They lay themselves upon the ground,
and as their spirits filter through the earth,
the brown grains soothe their mouths' complaints
and form a poultice for the brow like earth refining sugar,
and they can reconcile themselves to the snug berth.

Above,
tall gravestones shimmering with Hebrew words
shift slightly and accept another to the City of the Dead.
We look on and see that they belonged, not to us,
but to their generation
and their memories.

Sadness

Gathering
In the other room,
they are weeping, for the dead child—
grandmothers whose children
are still here,
and the young mother
whose child is gone.

The Funeral
Wind gentles the green branches,
flies up and parts the clouds
while blue sky stretches wide
beyond our view.
But we are a crowd
focused on
 too small a casket
underneath the flickering shade,
watching the father
kneel to let his tears fall
on the little box.

Shiva
Frame the house in black.
Blot out the mirrors' light.
Let the darkened porch
retreat from sight,
the lamp posts and the trees
hung with torn crepe
cease to reflect the shrouded stars.
While we wonder
In the next disordered days
that morning dares
to bring the sun's bright rays.

Alisa

Beautiful head
ready for sculpting on a long frame.
She disappeared into the kitchen
    to steam milk for the coffee
and with a flourish
brought it out on a teak tray with wafers;
talking all the while, her Viennese lilt
trilled over the partition
to remind us of an article in the Village Voice
or the Jerusalem Post on thin crackly paper.

Why did she sew, this intellectual?
I think she was exploring matter
and relationships
       as abstract as any philosophic text.

She cooked
relishing foods but savoring especially
the feat.
Sent away for tickets,
with every piquant offering clipped out and posted.

So many dinners
where the arabesque of talk fringed the severe living room
and we dined on white formica
garnished brilliantly.

II.

Why did she choose the ecstasy of death?
    Abandon home, husband, friends
    And her own next steps?

Did she believe it was her destiny
to try her mother's fate?
Did she prepare the way to be alone,
step behind pillars
to rehearse disappearance?
Play and replay the scene
until it must be done?

Goaded all the while
by the pain
of events that happened in the first month,
    tied down in the crib
      so she wouldn't bite her nails,
and crying,
        crying
through the dreams of night.

III.

We went to the green elmed cemetery.
Our first visit.
Couples came hand in hand
but did not see the others
    through tears
    that made a river
    washing away the circle of friendships
    like furniture in a flooded room
    once placed in harmony
    but driven helter-skelter through the door;

lost forever from that room,
            the objects
            and the half-conscious reasons
            they had been arranged so.

Such a green day
with mist rising from an earthy breath.
   Was the air made visible by knowing that there was a last time
            to see it?
   Did we first learn that green things are not in the dreams of death?

The couples gathered,
   choreographed for a stage production
   and felt constrained.
Alisa would have loved it though.
Had she not called it up
knowing
        we would write a script ourselves?

Gabi talked
loud enough for us to hear inside ourselves,
of pain, fear, accomplishment and peace.
He said, we stand here mourning
and a shudder passes deep through us
wondering who will follow.
Each one asks,"Will I do that, Will it be me?"

Monroe sang *El mole rahamim*
strong and clear
so we knew it had been done.

        Loudly calling:
        Let the elms hear, a Jew has died.
        Let the sky hear, and thunder come.
        Let the green leaves turn to brown, it is no trifle.
            Let this day shudder, a friend has died.

It was only fitting that he should bear
   your burden twice, Alisa,
find you dead —then be your messenger;
thus do we use our friends.

Anton, her father,
an unaccustomed yarmalka on his head,
wondered sardonically,
                      what is this—a wedding?

And the children—
faces white, unreadable,
books writing themeslves inside
   the crevasses of their souls,
enough material to stock a thousand plays.

"We'll see, we'll see."

Ceremonies ended,
words ceased.
The pine box pressed splinters
in our eyes.
Could we believe what was inside?
We rearranged the steps to this event.
   Prose would make it comprehensible, we thought.
No good,
the box descended
and grief accompanied the lowering.
We sobbed
each for an earlier burying
                      that taught us how to mourn.

IV.

Everyone else
felt guilty.
Did you know
I was more selfish than the rest,

      would not forgive,
      nor even take your part
      and cherish peace for your long agony.

Cannot forgive
the golden afternoons I lost
   although you lost a life.
Rage, my response
              that you should leave.
It's ten years afterwards
and I could still
rip through the coffin's lid
and shake you
              till your head fell off
its rotting body
and make the dried scissor wounds
     in your neck
bleed for the last time.

Consolation

Between the living and the dead
A mountain looms
Thick with pines
        Smooth high trunks and needle topping.

The dead float through this forest
And the trees comb us from them
Separating time from time, making memories begin.

Let them go, let the dead go. Let them draw away from our embrace,
Trailing hands along our arms, down to the fingertips.
And let them leave us empty of themselves.
Can you hear silence? Or a far-off wind? But no more conversation or debate.
Not even how they met their death, a subject that would interest them, is theirs.

Where childhood lives in us, they speak. Still powerful, they visit us in dreams,
And we relive our past in the magic shelter of a childhood room.
But waking, we shrink from the disloyalty indifference would proclaim.
Fear to lose the memory of face and voice.
Fear to erase ourselves, if senses fail to bring those words to mind
                                          as fresh messages.

Magnified and sanctified
Is the name of the Lord
Who makes Spring flowers and the season of farewells.

Magnified and sanctified is the name of God
Who gives life.
And though the tongue can hardly bear to form the words, nor eyes to look,
Nor tears to stop,
Blessed be the Lord who takes life, after a measure,
And turns the earth again, through rain, through green,
      White of snow,
           Toward many tomorrows.

Daryl Hafter spent her early years moving between the east and west coasts before her family finally landed in a suburban New Jersey Utopian colony called Free Acres. She blames having had five different grammar schools for her faulty arithmetic but praises Free Acres for her love of nature. A Henry George single-tax colony of some 90 residents, its core feature was awarding free leaseholds to creative people.

In the early 1920s and 1930s, artists from New York flocked there to spend summers in the congenial wooded colony. When it gained year-round residents, its artistic presence persisted. Painters, writers, poets, and musicians were busy at work and in this inspiring environment, her teenage poems found a readily encouraging audience.

At Smith College, Daryl concentrated on the study of French history. After earning a Ph.D. at Yale University, she published three books, including *Women's Work in Preindustrial France*. Frequent trips to Spain with her late husband, a professor of Spanish literature, and her two children, opened another window of culture. And while teaching history at Eastern Michigan University and pursuing her research in French archives, she continued to write poetry. It may seem strange to be a poet and a historian at the same time. For Daryl, the two disciplines coincided; both focused on uncovering the essence of lived experience.

Daryl lives in Ann Arbor, Michigan, where she continues to write poems.

www.ingramcontent.com/pod-product-compliance
Lightning Source LLC
Chambersburg PA
CBHW042311150426
43198CB00006B/115